CW01151697

Original title:
The Stillness of Snow

Copyright © 2024 Swan Charm
All rights reserved.

Author: Linda Leevike
ISBN HARDBACK: 978-9908-52-122-0
ISBN PAPERBACK: 978-9908-52-123-7
ISBN EBOOK: 978-9908-52-124-4

A Shimmering Pause in the Cold

Snowflakes dance, soft and light,
A hush descends, day turns to night.
The world at rest, a tranquil scene,
In winter's grasp, we find the sheen.

Branches draped in crystals glow,
Whispers of wind in breezes slow.
Time stands still, a breath held tight,
A shimmering pause, pure and bright.

The Unspoken Language of Winter

Silence speaks in frosted breath,
Underneath the icy wreath.
Footprints left in powdery snow,
Echo tales that only grow.

The trees weave secrets in the cold,
Timeless stories, softly told.
In the chill, we start to see,
The warmth of heart, unspoken glee.

Serenity Found in White

Fields of white, a blank canvas,
Nature's peace in its vastness.
Quiet moments, dreams take flight,
Wrapped in solace, pure delight.

Gentle flakes, so soft, so bright,
Covering chaos, bringing light.
In this beauty, we all find,
A serene stillness, intertwined.

An Ode to Frozen Moments

Icicles hang like crystal tears,
Moments frozen, held for years.
Each breath forms a fleeting cloud,
Nature whispers, soft and loud.

Captured time in shapes of glass,
Memories that forever last.
In the cold, we hold our dreams,
An ode to life, or so it seems.

Frozen Reverie

In winter's grasp, the world is still,
A blanket thick, white as a hill.
Silence drapes the sleeping ground,
In frozen dreams, peace can be found.

The trees wear coats of shimmering frost,
Each breath a cloud, warmth nearly lost.
Whispers of snowflakes softly fall,
Nature's quiet, a soothing call.

Beneath the stars, all is serene,
A tranquil realm, a glistening sheen.
Time pauses here, as moments freeze,
In chilling air, the heart finds ease.

The moon's pale glow bathes all in light,
Guiding the dreams of the gentle night.
In twilight's arms, the world's aglow,
A frozen reverie, soft and slow.

Snowflakes in a Quiet Dance

Whirling gently from the sky,
Snowflakes twirl, as they float by.
Each one unique, a work of art,
Falling silently, they play their part.

A delicate waltz upon the breeze,
They dance with grace among the trees.
Whispers soft, they kiss the ground,
In their descent, joy is found.

Frosted petals, light as air,
Carpeting earth with tender care.
In harmony, they softly gleam,
Transforming the world like a sweet dream.

The hush of winter wraps us tight,
As snowflakes echo through the night.
With every swirl, a story weaves,
In this quiet, the heart believes.

Muffled Footsteps on Crystal Streets

In the stillness, footsteps hush,
On crystal streets, where shadows brush.
Every sound, a muffled note,
In winter's cloak, the world remote.

Snow beneath, a soft embrace,
Each step, a dance in a timeless space.
The streetlights twinkle, casting gold,
Tales of winter quietly told.

Breath appears like fleeting smoke,
A moment's pause, the silence spoke.
With every crunch, the echoes blend,
A melody the night will send.

The air is crisp, with secrets old,
Winter's grace, a sight to behold.
In muffled footsteps, stories bloom,
On crystal streets, we find our room.

The Hush Before Twilight

As daylight fades, the world slows down,
Colors shift in a pastel gown.
In the silence, nature sighs,
A breathless pause beneath the skies.

The trees stand tall, a watchful sight,
As shadows blend with coming night.
Birds find nests, their songs now cease,
In this moment, we find our peace.

Crickets chirp, the stars awake,
A canvas bright for dreams to take.
In whispers soft, the twilight calls,
As quiet wraps around us all.

Time suspends in twilight's glow,
A gentle hush, the world below.
In this calm, we find our way,
In the hush before the end of day.

A Quiet Diary of Snowfall

The flakes descend without a sound,
Whispers of winter touch the ground.
Each flurry tells a tale so sweet,
A soft embrace where two worlds meet.

The trees stand still, a silent line,
Shadows merge as day declines.
In twilight's glow, the white unfolds,
A diary of dreams in gentle holds.

Footsteps echo in the hush,
Time slows down in the soft rush.
Every breath leaves a trace of steam,
In this serene, snowy dream.

Tracks lead on through frosted fields,
Nature's secrets softly yield.
Underneath the blanket bright,
Lies a world both pure and white.

The night descends, the stars ignite,
Filling the sky with silver light.
Snowflakes dance, a delicate show,
In this quiet diary of snow.

In the Embrace of Winter's Quiet

Soft whispers of the falling frost,
In winter's hold, we count the cost.
The world slows down, a breath held tight,
In the embrace of the soothing night.

Moonlight drapes the landscape wide,
In this stillness, hearts abide.
Crystals shimmer, a perfect scene,
Wrapped in silence, calm and serene.

The air, alive with crisp delight,
Each frozen branch dressed up in white.
Nature bathes in slumber's song,
In winter's low, where dreams belong.

As twilight fades to starlit views,
The world dons its midnight hues.
In every corner, peace resides,
In the calm where winter abides.

A flicker of warmth in the cold,
Moments captured, stories told.
In the heart of night's embrace,
We find the softest, safest place.

Painting Stillness on a Frozen Canvas

Blankets wide of glistening white,
The earth is hushed beneath the night.
A canvas drawn by nature's hand,
Each crystal stroke, a silent band.

The pines stand tall, cloaked in grace,
In frosted beauty, a timeless place.
In every corner, silence reigns,
While peace and calm flow through our veins.

Colors fade in the coming dusk,
As winter's chill awakens trust.
We wander through this tranquil maze,
Lost in wonder, caught in a daze.

Footprints soft on snow's embrace,
Each step taken, a gentle trace.
The world around, a wonderland,
A stillness felt, a dream so grand.

With every breath, the air is pure,
A symphony that's strange yet sure.
In winter's hold, we find the light,
Painting stillness in the night.

A Soft Breath of Chilled Air

A breath escapes, so crisp and clear,
In chilled air, winter draws near.
The world is wrapped in shivering bliss,
As whispers of frost ignite a kiss.

The morning sun, a watchful eye,
Glistening flakes like gems in the sky.
Each branch adorned with icy lace,
Nature's art, a pure embrace.

Horizon painted in pastel hues,
Winter's palette, soft and true.
A gentle sigh, the trees bow low,
In the dance of the falling snow.

Breathless moments, a fleeting sight,
Wrapped in the beauty of pure white.
In this stillness, peace we share,
A soft breath of the chilled air.

As day gives way to star-studded skies,
The night whispers, and softly sighs.
We cradle the stillness, just aware,
Of a world transformed by cold air.

Crystal Lullaby in the Dark

Whispers of night in a gentle grace,
Stars glisten soft in their silvery place.
Moonlight dances on shadows cast,
Embracing the dreams of the weary past.

Crystals twinkle in the chilly air,
Drawing stories, secrets they share.
A serenade hums, soothing and low,
Ensuring the heart feels the warmth of the glow.

In silence, a melody drifts to the east,
Where worries and troubles find quiet release.
Each note a promise, a tender embrace,
In the hush of the night, find your safe space.

A blanket of dreams falls gently anew,
Painting the skies in shimmering blue.
Feel the calm as the world slips away,
Wrapped in the calm of this luminous sway.

Hold close the lullaby that cradles the dark,
Let it ignite in you a flickering spark.
In crystal reflections, let stillness reside,
As the night warms your heart and the shadows abide.

Shimmers of Ice on Silent Waters

Ripples of light on the frozen stream,
Where winter unfolds like a delicate dream.
A tapestry grows in shimmering hues,
Nature's palette, adorned in frost-kissed blues.

Beneath the veneer, life quietly sleeps,
As silence embraces the depth of its keeps.
Glistening edges where shadows entwine,
The whispers of ice tell tales divine.

Branches bow low, draped in white lace,
While the elements gather with elegant grace.
A moment of stillness, reflection so pure,
In this transient beauty, we find our allure.

Echoes of time in the shimmering sheen,
A canvas of cold where the heart feels serene.
Each glimmer a story, a laughter, a sigh,
As the stars gaze down from the velvet sky.

Let the silent waters cradle your fears,
In the shimmering dance, find solace through years.
For within this moment, peace sweetly lingers,
As nature's art welcomes you with soft fingers.

Echoes of Calm in a Frosted World

Crisp air whispers through branches bare,
A world wrapped in frosty, luminous care.
Echoes of calm in the hush of deep night,
Where shadows and silver together alight.

Footsteps are soft on the blanket of white,
As dreams take their flight in the still of the night.
Each breath a cloud in the crystal-clear air,
In moments of wonder, we stop and we stare.

Frozen whispers, the world seems to pause,
In the quilt of the season, there's beauty because.
The stars weave their stories, a tapestry bright,
While nature sings softly beneath the pale light.

With every heartbeat, the silence takes form,
As the chill in the air embraces like warm.
A symphony plays in the heart of the cold,
An echo of calm that never grows old.

In frost's delicate hand, we find our true peace,
A solace that lingers, a beautiful lease.
Let life's hurried rhythms drift into dreams,
In the calm of the snow, we weave tender beams.

A Quiet Canvas of Snowflakes

Each snowflake whispers a tale of its own,
In a quiet canvas where beauty is sown.
Delicate dancers in frosty ballet,
Painting the world in their magical way.

They twirl through the air, soft as a sigh,
A moment of wonder as they drift by.
Covered in silence, the earth holds a breath,
In this fleeting moment, we dance with the death.

A tapestry spun of crystalline grace,
Where nature's designs find a tranquil space.
Each flake a reminder of life's fleeting song,
In the quiet of winter, we all can belong.

Look closely and see all the patterns align,
As the snowflakes entwine like the dreams of divine.
They shimmer and shine in soft shades of white,
A quiet affirmation of winter's delight.

As the night deepens, let your heart soar,
In this magic of snow, find your spirit once more.
Embrace the calm with each flutter and fall,
In the quiet of snowflakes, we are part of it all.

Tranquil Scenes of Glimmers and Glade

In the stillness of dawn's light,
Whispers of mist begin to rise,
Glimmers dance on leaves so bright,
Nature sings soft lullabies.

The glade, a canvas of calm,
Where shadows play beneath the trees,
Each leaf a note, a gentle balm,
Carried by a tender breeze.

Sunbeams filter, warm and sweet,
Painting gold on emerald green,
The chirping birds compose a greet,
Life awakens, fresh and keen.

Rippling streams, a melody,
Flowing through the quiet scene,
Nature's simple symphony,
Where peace resides, serene and keen.

Petals of Ice Falling from Heavens

From the dark sky, whispers flow,
Petals of ice begin to fall,
Blanketing the world below,
A shimmering, silent call.

Each flake a story, unique and bright,
Dancing in the chilly air,
Cloaked in the beauty of soft white,
A fleeting gift, delicate and rare.

They carpet fields, the trees, the ground,
Transforming all in tranquil grace,
Where laughter of winter can be found,
Embracing the world in a gentle embrace.

Underneath the moon's soft stare,
The glisten draws the heart near,
In this cold, enchanting air,
All worries and troubles disappear.

A Whispered Invitation from Winter's Hold

Winter whispers in the night,
Inviting dreams to softly soar,
Under stars that twinkle bright,
A world transformed to seek once more.

Frosted branches, silver lace,
Hillsides blanketed in a glow,
Nature holds a sweet embrace,
With every flake, love's gentle flow.

Fireplaces crackle, warm and near,
While outside, silence holds its reign,
In the stillness, winter dear,
Awaits the spring's unyielding gain.

A whispered promise, soft and clear,
In the hush, new stories bloom,
Winter's hold, a cherished cheer,
As life awaits with sweet perfume.

Harmonies of White in Frosty Air

In the frosty air, so clear,
Harmonies of white emerge,
A world adorned, serene and sheer,
Nature's beauty, a gentle surge.

Snowflakes twirl, a ballet grand,
Each one twinkles, soft and bright,
Covering all, a wonderland,
Blanketed in a soft twilight.

Pines sigh softly, dressed in white,
Moonlight glimmers on the stream,
A tranquil vision, pure delight,
Weaving dreams, a magic dream.

In this hush, the heart can sing,
With every breath, a calm embrace,
In winter's arms, we feel the spring,
As nature finds its gentle place.

Hushed Footsteps on Crystal Streets

Each step whispers secrets low,
On streets where softest breezes blow.
Moonlight glistens, a silver thread,
Guiding shadows where dreams are fed.

Footsteps dance on frosted ground,
Echoes of silence, profound.
The world holds its breath in the night,
Wrapped in magic, pure and bright.

Low murmurs of the icy air,
Trace tales of those who wander there.
Stars watch closely from their heights,
Stitching darkness with twinkling lights.

Hushed are the voices, soft as sighs,
Underneath the vast, velvet skies.
As time meanders, slow and sweet,
Whispers linger, where heartbeats meet.

In this calm, our spirits soar,
Each footstep leads to something more.
Paths of crystal, dreams untold,
Lay before us, rich as gold.

Slumbering Earth Beneath a Cotton Blanket

Beneath the snow, the earth takes rest,
Cradled softly, nature's nest.
Cotton clouds, they gently weep,
Guarding all as they drift to sleep.

Whispers of winter linger near,
Filled with promises, pure and clear.
Each flake a tale from skies above,
Kissing the earth with tender love.

Quietude wraps the world in grace,
As dreams unfold in this sacred space.
Life waits, hidden beneath the cold,
Embracing secrets yet to be told.

Branches bow with gentle weight,
Lost in a moment, a tranquil state.
Time stands still, as shadows blend,
In the arms of night, where slumber bends.

Awakened by spring, it will arise,
Bringing life beneath the skies.
But now it rests, in pure delight,
Beneath the stars, wrapped warm and tight.

Moonlight's Caress on Frozen Fields

Moonlight glows on fields so wide,
Casting silver o'er the tide.
Whispers of frost in gentle sway,
Dance beneath the night's soft play.

Each blade of grass holds crystal tears,
Cradling dreams of nameless years.
In this stillness, magic weaves,
A tapestry that nature leaves.

Shadows mingle with the light,
Painting stories of the night.
Every silence, rich and deep,
Speaks of secrets the stars keep.

Frozen breath, the world's soft sigh,
Underneath the endless sky.
Time meanders, softly bent,
In the glow of the moon's ascent.

Each moment stretched, a breath held tight,
Under the blanket of soft night.
Here in stillness, dreams take flight,
Carried onward through the light.

Time Paused in a Glacial Embrace

In the stillness, time stands still,
Frozen moments, a heavy thrill.
Glacial whispers touch the air,
Wrapped in silence, pure and rare.

The landscape breathes in icy grace,
Each glimmer holds a vast space.
Horizon merges with the skies,
Where dreams and echoes harmonize.

Footprints vanish, soft and slow,
Coated in white from above they glow.
Within this breath, the heart can see,
The gentle pull of reverie.

Nature's canvas waits in peace,
As icy fingers soothe and tease.
Time finds comfort in the chill,
Wrapped in moments, quiet and still.

The glacial glow, a tender pause,
In this serenity, there's no cause.
Lost in splendor, we embrace,
The tranquil joy of this still space.

Moments Encased in Frozen Delight

In the stillness of a winter night,
Stars twinkle, pure and bright.
Snowflakes dance in silent flight,
Each one a moment, soft and light.

Breath escapes like whispers cast,
Holding tight to shadows past.
Echoes linger, memories last,
In this frozen world, unsurpassed.

Hearts entwined in frosty air,
A snapshot of love, laid bare.
Warmth ignites amid the glare,
Moments cherished, none compare.

Wonders woven in icy threads,
Silent stories that warmth spreads.
Each embrace, a tale that weds,
Frosted dreams where joy treads.

The dawn arrives with gentle grace,
A light that brightens every face.
Memories clad in white lace,
In frozen delight, we find our place.

Slumbering Memories Under the Frost

Underneath the snowy sheet,
Lie whispers of the past, discreet.
Each flake holds a tale so sweet,
In dreams that long for time to greet.

Visions dance in quiet glows,
Echoes of the life that flows.
Beneath the frost, a warmth still grows,
In slumbering memories, love shows.

Winds of change, they softly sigh,
Carrying wishes as they fly.
Time melts gently, bids goodbye,
With every tear, a silent cry.

Holding tight to fleeting days,
In frozen stillness, love conveys.
Moments cherished in subtle ways,
We find warmth in winter's gaze.

Awake we rise from dreams so deep,
Where memories in silence keep.
In every snowdrift, promises seep,
As slumbering stories start to leap.

Shadows Melt into Winter's Embrace

As twilight falls, shadows begin,
Wrapped in winter's softest skin.
A chill surrounds, yet warmth within,
In every breath, a new day's spin.

A lantern glows on frosted lanes,
Whispers carried through snowy chains.
Each step forward, love remains,
In winter's grasp, our hope sustains.

Stars peek through the evening drape,
Crafting stories, a silent tape.
In icy realms, our hearts escape,
Shadows melt, as dreams reshape.

The world adorned in silver hues,
Beneath the frost, our spirit renews.
United hearts, the warmth imbues,
In winter's embrace, love pursues.

Fingers entwined, we walk the night,
In every corner, joy ignites.
Together, we conquer the frostbite,
With shadows fading, love takes flight.

The Chill of Time Encapsulated

In the stillness, time does freeze,
Moments caught with gentle ease.
Winds whisper secrets through the trees,
Each memory, a winter breeze.

Silhouettes of laughter echo near,
Through frosted panes, our dreams appear.
In this chill, we hold dear,
The essence of love, crystal clear.

Frosted nights with glowing light,
Moments cherished, hearts take flight.
The world outside, a sheer delight,
Encapsulated in pure white.

Time reflects in frozen streams,
Holding close our hidden dreams.
Through the cold, a warmth redeems,
In every sigh, love quietly beams.

The dawn breaks soft, a muted hue,
Awakening the world anew.
In winter's chill, we find what's true,
In every heartbeat, love's debut.

Portraits of Winter's Stillness

In quiet woods, the shadows lay,
Beneath the frost, the branches sway.
A silence hangs, so deep, so clear,
Each breath of cold is close and near.

The whispers of the swirling snow,
Tell tales of peace, a soft and slow.
When stars alight on frozen streams,
Their glimmer paints the night with dreams.

The world is hushed, a tender sigh,
As winter weaves a lullaby.
With every flake, a moment still,
A portrait brushed with nature's will.

The Enchantment of Silent White

The snowflakes dance in gentle flight,
Transforming earth to purest white.
A canvas stretched, so vast, so wide,
Where dreams of winter softly hide.

In every drift, a story told,
Of frosted skies and nights so cold.
The silence wrapped in silver sheen,
Unveils a world where few have been.

As twilight falls, the shadows grow,
The magic swirls in flakes of snow.
Each breath of air, a crystal spark,
Ignites the calm in winter's dark.

Tranquility in Frosted Traces

Upon the ground, a soft embrace,
Each step we take leaves but a trace.
The stillness deep, a soothing balm,
Where all is hushed, and hearts feel calm.

The trees stand tall in frosted grace,
Adorned with pearls, they hold their place.
The world transforms in silver glow,
A tranquil dance, a gentle flow.

In every breath, the crispness clings,
As winter's hand, in silence, sings.
A moment pure, a soft delight,
In tranquil dawn's first breath of light.

Imprints on a Softly Blanketed World

The snow lays thick, a quilted sheet,
With gentle curves beneath our feet.
Each footprint leaves a story spun,
In winter's grasp, beneath the sun.

The world feels new, a fresh surprise,
As breath becomes a misty rise.
The colors fade to monochrome,
Yet beauty thrives, as we roam home.

The whispers of the frozen air,
Entwine with dreams we long to share.
In every layer, life unfolds,
Imprints of warmth in winter's cold.

Softly Etched in Ice

A whisper glides on stillness here,
Patterns forming, pure and clear.
With every breath, the world does freeze,
Nature's art, a quiet tease.

Crystals glimmer under the moon,
Holding secrets, a soft tune.
Footsteps crunching on the ground,
Echoes linger, softly found.

Branches draped in glittering white,
Transform the day into the night.
Fragile moments, fleeting fast,
Frozen memories that will last.

Underneath this cold embrace,
Life persists at a slower pace.
Each frosted flake, a fleeting kiss,
In winter's grace, we find our bliss.

As dawn approaches, colors blend,
Softly etched, where shadows mend.
In this stillness, hearts ignite,
In frozen dreams, we find our light.

Winter's Blanket of Silence

Blanketing earth in a hush,
Snowflakes fall, the world a rush.
Whispers travel through the trees,
Carried softly by the breeze.

Footprints lead to places far,
Guided by the evening star.
Silent echoes fill the air,
Every moment, calm and rare.

Wrapped in layers, tender grace,
Embraced by winter's soft embrace.
Stories whispered, time stands still,
Serenity, a perfect thrill.

Fires crackle, shadows dance,
In the glow, we take a chance.
Hearts entwined in warm delight,
Winter's magic, pure and bright.

With each breath, the world ignites,
Crafting dreams on endless nights.
Under blankets, cozy, tight,
Silent joy in winter's light.

Gentle Caress of Frosted Dreams

Morning dew like glassy pearls,
Shimmering in the softest swirls.
Frosted whispers touch the ground,
In quiet love, they wrap around.

As daylight breaks, the chill retreats,
Warmth emerges, soft and sweet.
In the still, a promise grows,
Gentle caress, the magic flows.

Trees adorned in icy lace,
A fleeting moment, nature's grace.
Dancing shadows softly play,
Guiding hearts as night turns day.

Winter's breath, a tender kiss,
In the silence, find your bliss.
Dreams unfurl like all that's free,
In frosted realms, just you and me.

As stars twinkle in the dark,
Sharing secrets, love's sweet spark.
With every sigh, we find our way,
In winter's heart, we choose to stay.

Shadows Playing in Winter's Glow

As daylight fades and shadows creep,
The world retreats, as night falls deep.
In silver light, the whispers sway,
A dance of shadows, bright and gray.

The trees cast nets where spirits play,
In twilight's glow, they softly sway.
A flicker of warmth on skin so cold,
Tales of winter's heart unfold.

The moon above, a guardian bright,
Watches over the silent night.
Frosted whispers in the air,
In every corner, magic rare.

Footsteps crunch on snowy white,
Echoing softly in the night.
Each shadow shapes a fleeting dance,
In winter's glow, we take our chance.

Held in breath, the world slows down,
Shadows weave a radiant crown.
In winter's arms, we find our way,
In fleeting shadows, let us stay.

Still Fragility of Frozen Moments

In stillness hangs a fragile breath,
Moments captured, echoing death.
The world a canvas, blank and pure,
In frozen time, we find our cure.

A crystal lake reflects the sky,
Where dreams and whispers softly lie.
Each snowflake dances, bold and shy,
A fleeting touch, a silent sigh.

Time halts in frosty grasp of night,
Nurturing moments, secret and bright.
The hush of winter, sweet and deep,
In frozen corners, memories keep.

Yet in the chill, a warmth we find,
The beauty held in nature's mind.
Each frozen breath, a fleeting chance,
In still fragility, we advance.

As shadows fall, the heart beats slow,
In calm embrace, we learn to grow.
The world is still, yet full of sound,
In frozen moments, love is found.

Serenity in Flakes that Alight

Softly drifting, flakes descend,
A gentle touch, a quiet friend.
Each unique in its patterned flight,
Serenity found in winter's light.

Blanketing earth in quiet grace,
The world adorned, a snowy lace.
Silence speaks in whispers still,
In softest moments, hearts fulfill.

As flakes alight on outstretched palms,
A fleeting warmth amid the calms.
In every flake, a wish, a dream,
In winter's hold, life's tender stream.

The air is crisp, the night is young,
Nature hums an unvoiced song.
In solitude, it gently glows,
The peace that quiet winter knows.

Embrace the chill, let worries cease,
In falling flakes, we find our peace.
A simple moment, soft and bright,
Serenity lives in winter's light.

The Everlasting Quiet of Winter Hues

In winter hues, a stillness reigns,
The world transformed, where beauty gains.
Each color muted, soft as breath,
A canvas painted, life and death.

The skies are gray, a gentle shroud,
Wrapped in silence, beauty proud.
Footprints fade on icy ground,
In winter's quiet, peace is found.

The chill embraces every tree,
A breath of frost, a whispered plea.
In every branch, a story waits,
Of seasons past and future fates.

Hues of blue, the world a dream,
In endless quiet, shadows gleam.
Nature whispers truths untold,
In winter hues, life's grace unfolds.

As time stands still, we breathe it in,
The everlasting quiet begins.
In every moment, stillness flows,
In winter's calm, our spirit grows.

Serenity in a Snowbound World

Snowflakes tumble from the sky,
Blanketing the world so high.
Quiet whispers fill the air,
In this stillness, free from care.

Trees adorned in coats of white,
Glisten softly in the light.
Footsteps crunch on frozen ground,
In this silence, peace is found.

Birds nestle in their cozy homes,
While winter's chill softly roams.
A tranquil moment, pure and bright,
Serenity in the quiet night.

Stars twinkle in a velvet sky,
As the world seems to sigh.
Underneath this frosty dome,
In this chaos, we find home.

Nature sleeps, but dreams awake,
In every flake, a life we make.
In the calm, the heart can see,
The beauty of serenity.

A Stillness Cloaked in White

A quiet hush envelopes all,
As winter's blanket starts to fall.
Each flake a whisper, soft and light,
In the silence, hearts take flight.

Fields are draped in purest snow,
Transforming landscapes, row by row.
Frosted branches glow so bright,
In this charm of muted white.

The world slows down, a solemn grace,
As frosty fingers touch each place.
Time pauses in this frozen scene,
Where every breath feels fresh and clean.

Wonder dances in the night,
As shadows blend with pale moonlight.
Every corner holds a dream,
In the stillness, thoughts will gleam.

Softly now, the moments blend,
In this peace, all sorrows mend.
A stillness cloaked in white holds tight,
Promises of a new daylight.

Soft Shadows of Winter's Light

The sun dips low, a golden hue,
Casting shadows, twilight's cue.
Softly falling, dusk's embrace,
Surrounding all in gentle grace.

Winter's breath whispers through trees,
Swaying gently in the breeze.
Shadows stretch, a dance in flight,
Illuminated by fading light.

Every flake reflects the sun,
A world aglow, all is one.
In this calm, our hearts ignite,
With the soft shadows of winter's light.

Evening quiet, stars appear,
Cradling dreams, drawing near.
In the dark, a soft delight,
Woven in the fabric of night.

As the snowflakes gently fall,
Nature whispers, a tender call.
Together we embrace the sight,
Soft shadows guide our way tonight.

Frost's Lullaby

Whispers of frost fill the air,
Blanketing dreams, a gentle stare.
Each flake a note in winter's song,
Harmonies where all belong.

A cradle made of ice and snow,
Where hopes and wishes freely flow.
Nature's rhythm, soft and slow,
In this lullaby, hearts softly glow.

Mighty trees, adorned in white,
Stand as sentries in the night.
Their branches sway, a swaying dance,
In the moonlight's tender glance.

Frosted windows, warm inside,
Invite the dreams we cannot hide.
In the quiet, we drift away,
To frosty realms where children play.

So let the lullaby unfold,
As winter's magic takes its hold.
In frosty arms, wrapped up tight,
Serenading through the night.

Whispers of Winter's Breath

In the stillness, whispers float,
A chill that wraps like a soft coat.
Branches bare, in silence sway,
As winter breathes the light away.

Footprints mark the crisp white ground,
In this hush, peace can be found.
The air is sharp, yet sweet with pine,
Nature sleeps, in dreams divine.

Chimneys puffing clouds of gray,
As evening steals the light of day.
Frosted windows, tales untold,
Under blankets, hearts stay bold.

Snowflakes dance, a gentle cheer,
In the silence, love draws near.
A world painted in shades of light,
Winter whispers, soft and bright.

Silence Draped in White

The world is draped in a cloak so white,
Each breath a cloud in the fading light.
Snowflakes fall like gentle dreams,
In the hush, the heart redeems.

The trees stand tall, a frosty line,
Nature holds a still design.
In this calm, the shadows play,
Dusk embraces the end of day.

A blanket thick, it muffles sound,
In this realm, lost souls are found.
Whispered echoes fill the air,
Wrapped in silence, free from care.

Footsteps crunch on a winding path,
Laughter sparkles in winter's bath.
Memories weave through crisp, cold air,
In the still, a tender prayer.

Through the night, stars shine so bright,
Guiding dreams, igniting light.
As dawn approaches, gold and gray,
Silence wraps the world in sway.

Frosted Dreams Amidst the Pines

Beneath the pines, the dreams take flight,
Frosted edges gleam in night.
A whisper brushes through the trees,
Carrying hope on a gentle breeze.

Moonlight scatters soft and white,
Turning shadows into light.
In the stillness, hearts can hear,
The silent song of winter's cheer.

Each breath a mist, a fleeting ghost,
In this quiet, we embrace the most.
Stars blink softly, night's embrace,
Frosted dreams find their place.

Footfalls lead through snow-kissed trails,
Whispers echo, the heart exhales.
A secret shared in the lonesome dark,
As winter paints its tender mark.

Among the pines, the world is still,
Wrapped in peace, a cosmic thrill.
Frosted dreams hold us tight,
In the arms of this serene night.

Ghostly Veil of Serene Nights

Beneath the veil of ghostly light,
Whispers float in the depth of night.
A silken shroud, soft and cold,
In winter's arms, stories unfold.

With every breath, the stillness grows,
In the shadows, tranquility flows.
The moon a guardian, calm and bright,
Casting dreams in a silvered flight.

Trees stand sentinel, bold and free,
Whispering tales to the dreaming sea.
In the depth of night, hearts commune,
Beneath the watchful gaze of the moon.

Frost clings to every silent bough,
Nature bows, the world takes a vow.
To cradle warmth in the frosty air,
In every moment, a gentle prayer.

As dawn breaks through the chilling haze,
A palette of colors, the sun's warm gaze.
But in the night, a treasure stays,
Ghostly whispers, winter's praise.

Tranquil Veils of Crystal Air

A whisper floats on gentle breeze,
Veils of crystal dance with ease.
Nature's breath, a soft caress,
In whispered tones, the world's finesse.

Underneath the azure dome,
Hearts entwine, they feel at home.
Every leaf, a perfect tune,
Lifting dreams beneath the moon.

Clouds of silver, soft and light,
Brush the edges of the night.
In the stillness, shadows play,
Chasing all the fears away.

Each moment glimmers, pure and bright,
Captured in this endless flight.
Echoes linger in the air,
Life unfolds without a care.

As twilight falls, the stars emerge,
Bringing peace, a quiet surge.
Wrapped in thoughts, we breathe and sigh,
In crystal air, our spirits fly.

The Calm of Winter's Cloak

Snowflakes drift like silent dreams,
Covering the world in creams.
A blanket soft and pure in sight,
The calm of winter whispers light.

Trees stand tall in silent grace,
Adorned with frost, a lovely lace.
The world transformed, a quiet spell,
In winter's hold, all is well.

Footsteps muffled, echoes fade,
In this stillness, peace is made.
Every breath, a plume of white,
Nature's magic, pure delight.

Morning break, the sun will rise,
Painting hues in winter skies.
Softly warms the chilly air,
As life awakens from its lair.

In this season, hearts embrace,
Finding joy in every space.
Wrapped in love, we face the chill,
In the calm, our spirits thrill.

Ethereal Silence in the Frost

In the hush of frosty morn,
Nature waits, a world reborn.
Silence drapes like a soft cloak,
In every breath, a whispered stroke.

Icy branches touch the sky,
With fleeting clouds that gently fly.
A moment held, serene and still,
Time suspended, bend to will.

Footsteps track the crisp white ground,
In this beauty, peace is found.
Frosted air, a gift divine,
Embracing hearts, forever thine.

Beneath the sun's embracing glow,
Magic stirs in every snow.
In quietude, our thoughts take flight,
Ethereal dreams ignite the night.

As twilight dances on the frost,
We gather all the warmth we've lost.
In gentle whispers, life bestows,
The silence blooms within us, grows.

A Day Wrapped in White

A canvas stretched in shimmering light,
Cloaked in wonders, pure and white.
Each flake falls, a tale to tell,
As winter weaves a magic spell.

Children laugh in frosty play,
Building hopes in snow's soft sway.
Imagination takes its flight,
In a world adorned in white.

Skaters glide on lakes now froze,
As nature holds its quiet prose.
Every glance, a moment's charm,
Wrapped in warmth, away from harm.

As daylight fades to evening's glow,
Stars awaken, beauty flows.
The moon bestows its silver sheen,
On the tranquil, white-draped scene.

In this day of soft embrace,
We find our joy, a timeless grace.
With every breath, we feel the bliss,
A day wrapped in white, we reminisce.

Frosted Sentinels Standing Tall

Frosted trees in silence sway,
Guardians of the winter's way.
Their branches draped in icy lace,
Standing tall with quiet grace.

In the distance, echoes clear,
Whispers of the frost appear.
Nature's art, a still embrace,
Frosted sentinels hold their place.

Beneath the weight of snow's still song,
Ancient souls, they linger long.
In this realm where shadows fall,
Together they stand, proud and tall.

With every flake that softly lands,
The world transforms at winter's hands.
A tapestry of white unfolds,
In frosty wonder, nature holds.

As twilight falls, the stars arise,
Glistening in the winter skies.
Frosted dreams in night so bright,
Sentinels stand in gentle light.

The Quiet Grasp of Winter

Winter creeps without a sound,
Wrapping earth in white around.
A hush descends on every hill,
The world awaits, so calm, so still.

Brittle branches, stark and bare,
Glisten softly in crisp air.
Nature holds its breath in grace,
Winter's time, a slow embrace.

Streams are frozen, fields asleep,
Secrets in the snowdrifts keep.
Time meanders, cold and slow,
Wrapped within the winter's glow.

Night descends with velvet skies,
Stars like diamonds, bright and wise.
In the darkness, whispers flow,
The quiet grasp of winter's glow.

Underneath the frozen crust,
Life awaits, as all things must.
In the stillness, hope will rise,
When winter fades, spring will surprise.

Nature's Softest Sigh

Amidst the woods, a shiver flows,
Snowflakes dance as cold wind blows.
Nature breathes in silver light,
Her softest sigh at day's twilight.

Every flake a whispered dream,
Gentle origins, delicate seam.
A moment captured, pure and bright,
Nature's sigh, the heart takes flight.

Branches bow with heavy grace,
Carrying winter's soft embrace.
In the stillness, peace abides,
Whispers soft where beauty hides.

Each step leaves a trace so light,
In this world of muted white.
Nature cradles time so nigh,
In her arms, the softest sigh.

As dawn breaks with blush and gold,
Stories of winter gently told.
Nature's sigh, forever near,
In every heartbeat, calm and clear.

The Serenity of Snow-Covered Pines

Pines wear coats of glistening white,
Standing firm in winter's light.
A tranquil scene, so pure, so bright,
In their presence, hearts alight.

Gentle whispers in the breeze,
Snowflakes fall from lofty trees.
Each branch a treasure, softly clings,
Serenity that winter brings.

Footprints trace the path below,
Wandering through the earth's white glow.
A moment still, a world confined,
In quietude, our souls unwind.

Beneath their boughs, the world is still,
Pine-scented dreams, a timeless thrill.
In this space where calm aligns,
We find solace among the pines.

Time stands still in a snowy trance,
Nature invites us to take a chance.
In the hush, our spirits dance,
The serenity of winter's glance.

A Silent Dance of Feathered Snowflakes

In the stillness, whispers glide,
Snowflakes twirl, a gentle ride.
Softly falling, a pure embrace,
Nature's grace in silent space.

Each flake unique, a fleeting sight,
Dancing softly, pure delight.
In winter's hush, they weave and spin,
A tapestry where dreams begin.

Covered paths, a glistening sheet,
Crystals twinkle beneath our feet.
In the quiet, the world seems new,
A secret kept, a tranquil view.

Silent symphonies fill the air,
Winter's magic, beyond compare.
As time stands still, our hearts take flight,
In the glow of the soft moonlight.

So let us cherish this fleeting dance,
In the chill, we find romance.
For in each flake, a story told,
A silent dance in threads of gold.

Harmony in Hushed White Layers

Layers deep, the silence grows,
Nature's art in purest clothes.
Frosted whispers, soft and bright,
In the stillness, hearts take flight.

Beneath the white, the world lays bare,
Hidden dreams float in the air.
Every flake, a note in song,
Sings a winter's tale so long.

Branches bend with frosted grace,
Nature's hand, a soft embrace.
In shadows deep, the peace ignites,
Hushed layers gleam under starlit nights.

Footsteps echo, tender tread,
In the soft white, stories spread.
With each movement, echoes play,
A melody of light and gray.

Harmony in this frozen time,
Underneath the snow, a rhyme.
Together in this winter scene,
We find beauty in the serene.

Gentle Echoes Under a Silver Sky

Beneath the sky, a silver hue,
Gentle echoes call to you.
A whisper soft, the night unfolds,
In moonlit dreams, our hearts hold gold.

Snow blankets the world in peace,
Silence reigns, all troubles cease.
In every flake, a story weaves,
As nature's breath softly leaves.

The air is crisp, the shadows dance,
In winter's glow, we take a chance.
To listen close, to feel, to know,
The gentle echoes of falling snow.

Each star glimmers, a note so bright,
In this serene, enchanted night.
The world asleep, in dreams we play,
In silver light, we drift away.

Wrapped in warmth, we cherish time,
Under whispers, sweet as rhyme.
For in each moment, love awakes,
Gentle echoes of snowflakes.

Footprints Lost in a Sea of White

Footprints trace a tale unseen,
In the white, where we have been.
Each step swallowed by the snow,
A world that whispers soft and slow.

Windswept paths where silence dwells,
Echoing softly, winter's spells.
As currents shift, we start to fade,
In the sea of white, memories laid.

Frosty breaths, the air so still,
Capturing time with a gentle thrill.
Yet in the hush, we learn to roam,
In this sea, we find our home.

Clouded visions, our paths entwined,
Lost in layers, warmth we find.
The footprints fade, but tales remain,
Of journeys shared through joy and pain.

Let us wander, hand in hand,
In a snow-filled, enchanted land.
For in these moments, we see the light,
Footprints lost in a sea of white.

A Canvas of Pure Tranquility

In morning's soft embrace, we wake,
The sun spills gold on leaves that shake.
A river flows with whispered peace,
Where time slows down and worries cease.

The trees stand tall, a timeless sight,
Beneath the sky, so vast and bright.
Birds sing sweetly, a gentle tune,
A dance of joy beneath the moon.

With every breeze, the world feels still,
A moment caught, a heart to fill.
The meadow blooms in colors bold,
A canvas rich with stories told.

In quiet corners, shadows play,
As light and dark weave through the day.
A cherished space, where dreams take flight,
In unity of peace and light.

With every breath, tranquility grows,
In nature's lap, where love bestows.
This haven found, a refuge clear,
A canvas drawn, forever near.

Winter's Gentle Caress

Snowflakes drift in soft descent,
A silent hush, as day is spent.
The world is wrapped in white so pure,
A tranquil gift, a heart's allure.

Branches bow beneath the weight,
As winter paints a quiet fate.
The air is crisp, a breath of chill,
A moment still, with time to fill.

Footprints mark the path we've tread,
While whispers of the past are spread.
In every flake, a story spun,
A fleeting kiss from winter's sun.

By fireside, the flames dance bright,
Casting warmth in coldest night.
With cocoa warm, our spirits rise,
As winter's magic fills the skies.

So let us savor this embrace,
In winter's arms, find our own place.
For in this chill, we find our rest,
In gentle caress, we are blessed.

Frozen Echoes of the Night

The moon hangs low, a silver sphere,
While shadows dance, the night draws near.
Cold whispers lace the starlit air,
As echoes call, a ghostly prayer.

Beneath the frost, the earth lies deep,
In stillness, secrets softly seep.
The world asleep, a muted sigh,
As frozen dreams drift gently by.

Each breath we take is crisp and clear,
A symphony that few can hear.
In darkness rich, old tales awake,
As time slips past, a haunting ache.

We wander through the snowy trees,
With every step, the heart agrees.
In frozen nights, our souls unite,
As echoes linger, pure and bright.

The stars align in quiet grace,
Reflecting all we dare embrace.
In night's embrace, we find our light,
In frozen echoes of the night.

Ghosts of Winter's Breath

The chilling winds begin to rise,
As winter comes with quiet sighs.
Ghostly forms in shadows roam,
In frozen landscapes, they find home.

With every flake that gently falls,
A whisper lingers, softly calls.
The trees, adorned in crystal lace,
Hold memories of a warm embrace.

The silent nights, so deep and wide,
In their expanse, the past can hide.
With every gust, a tale retold,
Of dreams long gone and hearts of old.

In frosted air, a shimmer glows,
As winter's breath the stillness knows.
A breathless pause in nature's song,
Where fleeting moments still belong.

So let us walk through realms of white,
With echoes dancing in the night.
In the ghosts of winter's breath we find,
The threads of time that bind us blind.

The Quietude of Falling Flakes

In gentle swirls, they dance and glide,
Perfect whispers where dreams reside.
Softly settling on branches bare,
A tender quilt beyond compare.

Each flake unique, yet all the same,
Silent magic, a timeless game.
Carpets woven with icy lace,
Nature's stillness, a warm embrace.

The world is hushed, the moment still,
Blanketed hills, a tranquil thrill.
In the evening's soft, fading light,
Snowflakes shimmer, reflecting night.

A hush descends, the air is clear,
The heart finds peace, the soul draws near.
In this quietude, solace flows,
As winter's beauty gracefully grows.

So let us cherish this fleeting scene,
In a world of white, serene and clean.
As falling flakes weave tales untold,
We find our warmth in winter's cold.

Silence Thrown Across the Landscape

A gentle hush invites the mind,
In snowy fields, pure peace we find.
The whispers fade, as shadows shift,
A tranquil spell, a beautiful gift.

Footsteps soft on powdery ground,
Nature's breath in silence found.
Underneath the vaulted sky,
Stillness reigns, as time slips by.

The trees stand tall, draped in white,
Guardians of this quiet night.
Each flake that falls a tale to tell,
In winter's grace, we dwell so well.

Moonlight dances on crystal streams,
Reflecting all our sweetest dreams.
Amid the calm, the spirit grows,
In silence thrown, the beauty flows.

Let us wander through this dream,
Where all is right and life's a gleam.
In the silence, hearts unite,
Across the landscape, pure delight.

Winter's Breath, Soft and Slow

Breath of winter fills the air,
With every gust, a gentle care.
As frost adorns the brittle ground,
A hushed enchantment wraps around.

The world transformed, a crystal dome,
A fleeting chill becomes our home.
In softest sighs, the moments pass,
Each breath a whisper, each sound a glass.

Swirling winds and snowflakes twirl,
In winter's grip, the senses whirl.
With every flake, a story weaves,
In soft embraces winter leaves.

Underneath a starry veil,
The night grows deep, a silver trail.
Comfort found in this embrace,
Nature's wonder, our sacred space.

So let us breathe in this still night,
In winter's hold, we find our light.
With every exhale, love will grow,
In the warmth of winter's breath, soft and slow.

Beneath a Shroud of Snow

A blanket white on earth's embrace,
Nature's canvas, a hushed place.
Beneath the shroud, the world asleep,
In tranquil depths, our dreams we keep.

Every branch draped in frosted lace,
In this quiet, we find our grace.
Footsteps muted on the trail,
In winter's tale, we softly sail.

With each soft flake that falls anew,
The world transforms in glistening hue.
Whispers flow in breezes mild,
In quietude, the heart is wild.

Moonbeams dance on frozen streams,
The night alive with silvery gleams.
Beneath the shroud, a promise glows,
In each still breath, the magic flows.

So here we pause, our spirits soar,
In winter's hush, we yearn for more.
Together wrapped in nature's care,
Beneath the snow, love's warmth we share.

Frost Kisses the Earth

Beneath the pale, soft light,
Frost glimmers on the ground,
Nature's breath, a silent sigh,
A magic dance, profound.

Trees wear coats of silver lace,
Branches bow with gentle grace,
Every step a cushioned sound,
In this icy world, we're bound.

Footprints trail like secrets told,
In whispers through the cold,
Each moment, a treasure clear,
In winter's grasp, we draw near.

Time slows down in crystal air,
Hearts awaken, feel the stare,
Of beauty wrapped in snowy white,
A tranquil pause, pure delight.

When evening comes, stars will gleam,
Painting shadows, a quiet dream,
Frost kisses earth with tender care,
In this stillness, love to share.

Hushed Whispers in a Winter Wonderland

Snowflakes fall like gentle prayers,
Hushed whispers float in frosty air,
Each flake a story softly spun,
In winter's realm, we all are one.

The world is wrapped in quiet peace,
A chill that brings a soul's release,
Footfalls muffled, heartbeats near,
In this wonderland, we steer.

Icicles dangle, twinkling bright,
A shimmering beauty in the night,
As shadows dance on drifts of white,
Each breath a cloud, pure and light.

Nights are longer, days are slow,
Yet warmth ignites where love can flow,
Together, we embrace the cold,
In this wonder, hearts unfold.

So let us wander hand in hand,
Through this beautiful, silent land,
With hushed whispers and dreams in flight,
In a winter's glow, we find our light.

Still Waters Beneath Winter Skies

Still waters mirror a sky of gray,
Where whispers of winter softly play,
Reflections dance in the quiet chill,
A beauty found in nature's will.

The trees stand tall, their branches bare,
Guardians of secrets they silently share,
Frozen stillness, a canvas pure,
Each moment here, we feel secure.

The world slows down, a tranquil pause,
In winter's grasp, we find our cause,
To cherish peace and silence rare,
In nature's arms, beyond compare.

Birds may sing, but soft and low,
In reverie, we learn to grow,
With every breath, the icy air,
We find a path, explore with care.

So let the waters guide our hearts,
Under winter's blanket, where love imparts,
Stillness reigns in the calm embrace,
In this quietude, we find our place.

A Pause in Time

Winter whispers like a soft refrain,
Moments linger, yet they wane,
A pause in time, a breath we take,
In frosty air, our hearts awake.

The snowflakes swirl, a gentle dance,
In their descent, we find a chance,
To savor every twinkling light,
In this season, pure and bright.

Beneath the stars, so vast and wide,
We lose ourselves in nature's tide,
Each flicker brings a memory clear,
In winter's arms, we have no fear.

Chill winds beckon, the night draws near,
But in this stillness, we feel no fear,
Wrapped in warmth, a cozy embrace,
Time freezes, leaving no trace.

So let us pause in the snowy glow,
With hearts aglow, let love bestow,
In gentle moments, we'll abide,
Together in winter's gentle stride.

Blanketed White

Blanketed white, the ground is dressed,
In winter's charm, we find our rest,
With each soft flake, a cover deep,
In silence, dreams and wishes sleep.

A canvas pure, untouched, so bright,
Transforming all beneath its light,
Footsteps trail like stories told,
In this wonderland, brave and bold.

The world, it sparkles, a diamond sheen,
In every corner, beauty is seen,
A fleeting pulse, the heart's delight,
Wrapped in magic of the night.

Grateful hearts find joy in white,
In beauty born from winter's bite,
Amidst the chill, warmth unfolds,
In these moments, love's worth gold.

So let us wander through this scene,
In the soft hush of evergreen,
With nature's gift, our spirits rise,
In winter's hold, we touch the skies.

Beauty Frozen in Time's Grasp

In winter's clutch, the world does pause,
A breath held tight, in stillness, we draw.
Each flake that falls, a whisper soft,
Crafting a quilt where dreams aloft.

Nature's canvas, white and pure,
Embracing cold, the heart's allure.
Here moments freeze, in icy sighs,
We find our peace 'neath tranquil skies.

A silent dance, with shadows played,
In the cool glow, memories laid.
Encased in frost, a timeless grace,
Beauty captured, in winter's embrace.

Time stands still as seasons change,
Each fleeting glance feels oh so strange.
In frozen gems, our stories lie,
And in their depths, we drift and fly.

With every chill that coats the ground,
In silence rich, our hopes are found.
For beauty rests in nature's rhyme,
Frozen forever, suspended in time.

A Symphony of Silence in Crystal

Upon the lake, a silence sings,
The frozen world, where winter clings.
Each breath a cloud, a fleeting mist,
In crystal realms, our dreams coexist.

Notes of stillness, sweet and clear,
As hushed tones linger, drawing near.
The wind whispers through barren trees,
A melody spun with perfect ease.

Icicles dangle, sharp and bright,
Reflecting shards of soft twilight.
Each glimmering edge, a silent sound,
In this serene, enchanted ground.

The pulse of frost, a gentle beat,
Nature's rhythm in quiet retreat.
In every moment, time stands still,
A symphony played by frost's sweet will.

As twilight wraps the world in gray,
A tranquil hush, the end of day.
Here in the stillness, hearts align,
In the symphony of silence, divine.

Lightly Layered Dreams of Ice

Frosted whispers, soft as dreams,
On distant hills, the sunlight beams.
Each layer thick, a tale untold,
In frozen realms, life's secrets hold.

The world transformed, a wondrous sight,
With gentle hues of blue and white.
Inside the crystal, shadows play,
In lightly layered, timeless display.

Beneath the surface, whispers churn,
A hidden warmth, waiting its turn.
In frozen stillness, dreams unfold,
With every layer, more to behold.

A child's laughter, crisp and bright,
Echoes gently in the fading light.
Each flake a glimpse, a fleeting glance,
A dance of dreams, a winter's chance.

So lift your eyes to skies so vast,
Where lightly layered hopes are cast.
In every frost, our dreams will rise,
A tapestry woven 'neath winter skies.

Unwritten Stories Beneath the Flurries

Snowflakes fall, like whispered tales,
On winds that weave like ancient sails.
Each twirling flurry, a chance to start,
Unwritten stories from the heart.

Below the drifts, the earth sleeps deep,
Where secrets lie, and shadows creep.
In every flake, a world anew,
Endless tales waiting for a clue.

The past may linger, soft and grey,
Yet in the snow, it fades away.
With every gust, we dance and play,
Writing new paths with dreams of today.

In winter's grasp, we pause to see,
The shimmering beauty, wild and free.
Each moment captured, a fleeting spark,
Dancing stories in the winter dark.

So let the snowflakes fall and flow,
To write the tales we long to know.
For beneath the flurries, life does bloom,
In unwritten stories, we find room.

A Tranquil White Silence

Softly falls the gentle snow,
Blanketing the world below.
Whispers dance in winter's breath,
Silence reigns, a hush of death.

Icicles hang like crystal tears,
Reflecting dreams, calming fears.
Stars peek through the evening gray,
Guiding lost souls on their way.

Barren trees wear coats of white,
Holding still in soft moonlight.
Nature breathes, a sacred pause,
In the stillness, we find cause.

Footsteps crunch on frozen ground,
Echoes of the peace profound.
Every flake a work of art,
Painting calm upon the heart.

As night deepens, shadows blend,
In this pause, we find a friend.
A tranquil night, vast and bright,
Wrapped in winter's pure delight.

The Peace of a Snow-Capped World

Snowflakes twirl in quiet grace,
Covering every rugged space.
Mountains wear their frosty crowns,
Guardians of the silent towns.

A hush hangs over fields of white,
Softly glowing in the night.
Footprints tell the tales of old,
In snowbound stories yet untold.

Pine trees sway with tender ease,
Whispers carried on the breeze.
Nature sleeps with dreams concealed,
In this canvas, peace revealed.

Moonlight dances on the snow,
Casting shadows to and fro.
Each radiance a sign to find,
The stillness wrapped in heart and mind.

In this world, the cares subside,
Joy found in the soft white tide.
The peace that winter's grace unfolds,
A solitude that gently holds.

Snowbound Meditations

In the quiet of the storm,
Thoughts gather, feelings warm.
Each flake a crystal thought defined,
Lost in winter, unconfined.

Sitting still with eyes closed tight,
Drifting through the soft, pale light.
Breath of winter, soft and deep,
In the snow, old dreams we keep.

Branches bow under frosty weight,
Silent moments that await.
Echoes whisper from the trees,
Carried on the chill of breeze.

Thoughts like snowflakes gently fall,
Every one a tender call.
In this still, reflective place,
We embrace the quiet grace.

As the world falls deep asleep,
Awake in dreams, our secrets keep.
In the snowbound lullaby,
We find peace beneath the sky.

Starlit Dreams on a White Canvas

Beneath the stars, a canvas bright,
Snowflakes shimmer in the night.
Whispers float in icy air,
Dreams emerge, weaving care.

Crystalline worlds of silver hue,
Reflecting what the heart holds true.
In this splendor, souls collide,
In the stillness, we confide.

Softly glow the starlit skies,
As night unfolds in whispered sighs.
Brush of frost on every tree,
Painting realms of memory.

In the silence, thoughts take flight,
Glimmers of a soft, pure light.
Every flicker, every gleam,
Tales of hope, a waking dream.

With each step, the shadows play,
Guiding us along the way.
In the dance of night and snow,
Starlit dreams begin to grow.

Embers of Quietude

Softly falling leaves trace the ground,
Whispers of the night softly abound.
A flicker of light escapes the dusk,
In these moments, silence we trust.

Beneath the stars, a peaceful glow,
The world slows down, its gentle flow.
Embers dance in quiet grace,
Holding secrets, a sacred space.

Moonlit shadows waltz and sway,
Dreams take flight, night turns to day.
In the stillness, heartbeats align,
Embers of quietude, truly divine.

Rippling waters speak in tones,
The cool breeze hums ancient bones.
Time stretches thin, a fragile thread,
In tranquil twilight, worries shed.

So let us linger in this embrace,
Lost in time and peaceful space.
The embers fade but never die,
In quietude, we learn to fly.

In the Arms of Winter

Snowflakes whisper secrets low,
Blanketing dreams with a soft glow.
In the arms of winter, we find,
A tranquil peace, a boundless mind.

Trees wear coats of glimmering white,
Stars dance in the deep of night.
Fires crackle, warmth bestowed,
In the arms of winter, hearts erode.

Paths wind through the icy haze,
Footsteps follow a timeless maze.
Each breath clouds in the chilly air,
In winter's arms, there's love to share.

Frosted windows paint the floor,
A canvas quiet, begging for more.
Each moment still, every sight dear,
In winter's arms, we conquer fear.

As days become shorter, warmth will rise,
Glow of the hearth, under open skies.
In the arms of winter, solace we'll find,
A gentle embrace, forever entwined.

Whispers on Crystal Peaks

Crystal peaks reach for the skies,
Murmurs of nature, softest sighs.
Whispers of wonders, the world below,
In the hush of mountains, secrets flow.

Wind carries tales, ancient and bold,
Through valleys deep, where stories unfold.
Footsteps echo on frost-kissed trails,
In whispers of crystal, magic prevails.

Beneath the twilight, shadows play,
Guiding lost souls, lighting the way.
The heartbeats of mountains, strong and deep,
In whispers on crystal, mysteries seep.

Stars peek through the veil of night,
Illuminating dreams in silver light.
Mountains stand guard, fierce and grand,
In whispers of crystal, destinies planned.

Embrace the quiet, the still of the air,
Whispers on crystal, a call to dare.
Journey on peaks, where spirits roam free,
In the gaze of the mountains, find the key.

Winter's Gentle Whisper

Gentle flakes drift from the skies,
Winter's breath, a lullaby sighs.
Each patch of snow, a blanket's embrace,
In winter's whisper, we find our place.

Crystals glisten in morning's light,
Dancing softly, pure and bright.
Frost kisses every branch and stone,
In winter's whisper, we're never alone.

A crackling fire warms the night,
Stories wrapped in a soft twilight.
Families gather, hearts intertwine,
In winter's whisper, love will shine.

The world slows down, in a serene hush,
Beneath the stars, we feel the rush.
Time drifts softly, a gentle stream,
In winter's whisper, live the dream.

So here we pause, each moment we're near,
In winter's embrace, there's nothing to fear.
A gentle whisper leads us on,
In love's warm glow, the snowflakes are gone.

Ghostly Silhouettes Against a Winter Canvas

In the quiet glade, shadows dance,
Figures emerge from winter's trance.
Silent whispers in frosty air,
Nature's breath, ethereal fair.

Branches bare, enshrined in white,
Eclipsed by the cold, fading light.
Footprints lost in layers of snow,
Ghostly secrets, they ebb and flow.

Moonlight casts an argent glow,
Painting portraits of the below.
Through trees, a shiver runs deep,
Ancient tales that time keep.

Against the backdrop, a spectral sigh,
As the night marches on, oh so sly.
In the stillness, stories unfold,
In hushed tones, the past retold.

Echoes of laughter, long since passed,
Frozen memories that forever last.
In winter's embrace, the spirits roam,
In this canvas, they find their home.

Frost's Embrace on Nature's Heart

Frost blankets the earth in jeweled lace,
Nature lies tranquil, wrapped in grace.
Each blade of grass, a crystal shard,
A silent symphony, sweet and hard.

Whispers of winter brush through the trees,
With a gentle touch that brings one to knees.
Under the breath of icy night,
Life holds its heartbeat, soft and light.

Brittle leaves crunch underfoot,
Revealing stories buried deep, uncut.
Time stands still in this frozen realm,
While frosty hands take at the helm.

The world shines bright, a shimmering sight,
As frost glimmers under the pale moonlight.
Nature's heartbeat slows to a sigh,
While the stars watch from the vast sky.

In the hush, all creatures retreat,
To find solace where earth and frost meet.
Beneath the hush, life quietly dreams,
In frost's embrace, the heart gleams.

Stillness Wrapped in Winter's Garment

Wrapped in stillness, a world pristine,
Winter cloaks the landscape, serene.
Snowflakes swirl in a delicate dance,
Nature's grace in a frozen romance.

The brook's soft murmur, now hushed and low,
Under layers of ice, it lies in slow.
Covered in fog, the horizon fades,
As daylight's touch gently evades.

Each quiet breath, a still exchange,
Life paused amidst the cold, so strange.
Time, like snow, gently drifts down,
Crowning the earth in a white gown.

Deer tread lightly on paths so new,
In search of warmth, a love so true.
In the depth of silence, secrets lie,
As shadows stretch beneath the sky.

Night descends with a velvet sigh,
A tapestry woven, both low and high.
Winter's garment, heavy and vast,
Encases the memories of times long past.

Soft Twilight Beneath a White Canopy

Soft twilight falls, a gentle hand,
Cradling the trees in a silken band.
Underneath this blanket, all is bright,
A hush weaves through the emerging night.

The world transformed in muted tones,
Whispers of night coax out the drones.
The stars peek shyly through branches bare,
Curtains of frost swirl in the air.

Snowflakes twinkle in the dying light,
Each a messenger from the night.
In this peace, all troubles cease,
As night finds solace, offering peace.

A lullaby of shadows start to play,
Crickets hush, the day drifts away.
Beneath the canopy, dreams take flight,
In the tender embrace of falling night.

With every breath, the world holds tight,
To the tenderness of winter's flight.
In this moment, all hearts unite,
Under soft twilight, a pure delight.

Whispers of Frosted Dreams

In the hush of night, whispers call,
Softly weaving through the hall.
Stars twinkle bright in the silvery sky,
Frosted dreams dance, shimmering high.

Each breath a cloud, each thought a breeze,
Crystals gather on the bending trees.
Night's gentle song, a lullaby sweet,
Guides us as slumber and magic meet.

The world is hushed, asleep in white,
Wrapped in dreams 'neath the pale moonlight.
Footsteps muffled in the soft, cold air,
Whispers of frost, a spell we share.

Snowflakes twirl in a timeless waltz,
Each one unique, it never halts.
They blanket the earth, a tender cloak,
Whispers of frost, the winter spoke.

Awake to wonder, to beauty's gleam,
In the heart of winter, we dare to dream.
Every twinkling star, every frosty gleam,
Calls us to dance in this frosted dream.

Silent Blankets of White

Silent blankets embrace the ground,
Cocooning the world in a soft, white sound.
Trees wear their coats of glistening snow,
In this quiet hush, the magic flows.

Winter nights hold a secret grace,
Under the cover, a tranquil space.
Whispers of cold breathe life anew,
In the silence, old dreams break through.

Footprints trace stories from where we've been,
Marking the passage of moments unseen.
Each flake a promise, each drift a sigh,
Silent blankets of white, let time fly by.

Children's laughter, a gleeful cheer,
As they sculpt magic in the atmosphere.
Snowmen rise with smiles so bright,
Against the canvas of sheer white night.

In the stillness, the world takes pause,
Wrapped in beauty without a cause.
Echoes of joy in the frosty air,
Silent blankets of white, we cease to care.

Where Icicles Hold Their Breath

Where icicles dangle, glistening clear,
Hanging like gems, drawing us near.
Each drip a moment, suspended in time,
Whispers of winter, a haunting rhyme.

Frozen fingers of frost touch the pane,
Painting scenes where treasures remain.
Nature's artistry, a captivating sight,
Where icicles hold their breath at twilight.

Amidst the stillness, a heartbeat calls,
Echoing softly through snowy halls.
In this frozen realm, dreams arise,
Reflecting the wonder in frost-bitten skies.

Lingering shadows paint pathways bold,
Stories of winter, quietly told.
Nature's canvas, serene and bright,
Where icicles hold their breath in the night.

Silence perfumed with the chill of the wind,
Whispers of frost in the chill rescind.
Magic unfolds with each step we tread,
In this realm where icicles dream instead.

Serene Silence of Winter's Embrace

In the gentle hush of twilight's glow,
Winter wraps the world in a soft, white flow.
Branches bow low under blankets of snow,
Serene silence whispers, sweet and slow.

Frost-kissed fields undulate like waves,
Carried by breezes that hush and save.
Each flake a door with stories inside,
In winter's embrace, our worries abide.

Night falls softly as shadows dance,
In the moon's cool light, we find romance.
Each moment a blessing, pure and bright,
As we cradle warmth 'neath the velvet night.

Through frosty windows, we gaze afar,
Yearning for dreams as bright as a star.
Serenity wrapped in a tranquil grace,
Winter's deep magic, a warm embrace.

Let us walk softly through this gentle land,
Hand in hand, where silence expands.
In the serene silence, our spirits trace,
The beauty of winter's sweet embrace.

The Quiet Kiss of Winter's Hand

The trees stand bare, in silence deep,
A blanket white, where shadows sleep.
Snowflakes dance in soft descent,
Whispers of cold, where warmth once went.

Frosted breaths from lips of night,
Every corner shimmers bright.
Nature's breath, a still refrain,
Echoes lost, yet felt again.

The world adorned in icy lace,
Time slows down, we find our place.
In winter's clutch, we pause to rest,
A moment's peace, the heart's sweet quest.

Each step cracks underfoot, a sound,
In this hushed realm, all joy is found.
The quiet kiss of winter's hand,
A solace drawn from nature's strand.

As evening falls, the stars appear,
In this landscape, we hold dear.
The whispers of the winds do call,
In winter's hush, we feel it all.

Unseen Tales in the Snow's Soft Whisper

Beneath the veil of glistening white,
Stories sleep away from sight.
Footprints lost, yet memories stay,
In snow's embrace, they softly play.

The trees may sway, but whispers hold,
Secrets of winter, quietly told.
Each flake descends with tales to weave,
In silence deep, we must believe.

A rabbit hops, a fleeting ghost,
In this pristine world, we can boast.
The earth wears tales of ages past,
In snow's soft grip, our hearts beat fast.

Every shimmer holds a spark,
Of lives lived out from dawn till dark.
Unseen tales in the snow's soft breath,
We find ourselves within this depth.

As twilight hugs the fading light,
Hope shines through the snowy night.
In this quiet, we sink and flow,
Finding peace in the gentle snow.

Night's Gentle Breath on Frosted Blooms

Under the moon's tender gaze,
Frosted blooms in a gentle haze.
Night's caress, so soft, so light,
Whispers secrets, dims the sight.

Petals freeze with dreams untold,
A beauty in the night so bold.
Each bloom shimmers, a breath of grace,
In shadows deep, we find our place.

The stars above, like scattered gems,
Kiss the flowers at night's end.
Silent stories in the air,
Trace of warmth, a wishful prayer.

In this moment, time stands still,
Night's gentle breath, a soothing thrill.
Under starlit skies, we roam,
Among the blooms, we find our home.

As dawn approaches, frost may flee,
But memories linger, wild and free.
Night's gentle breath, forever near,
In every bloom, a whispered cheer.

A Dreamscape of Stillness Beneath the Stars

Under a dome of twinkling light,
We wander softly through the night.
A dreamscape painted in silver hue,
Where silence reigns and time feels new.

The moon hangs low, a watchful eye,
As echoes of night begin to sigh.
Each star above holds tales to share,
In this moment, we lay bare.

The crisp air whispers through the trees,
Carrying secrets on the breeze.
As shadows linger, we reflect,
In stillness found, we reconnect.

A universe vast, our hearts align,
In nature's arms, our spirits shine.
A dreamscape rich with hopes and fears,
Born from laughter, grown from tears.

As night gives way to dawn's embrace,
We hold this peace, our sacred space.
Beneath the stars, our souls expand,
In this stillness, we take our stand.

The Blanket of Calm in a Frozen Realm

In the hush of snow's embrace,
A stillness wraps the quiet place.
Each flake a whisper, soft and pure,
Nature rests, serene and sure.

Beneath the stars that twinkle bright,
Love unfurls in the soft night.
Branches bear the weight of dreams,
Silent echoes, tender beams.

Footsteps muffled, soft and slow,
In this realm where calm doth flow.
Beneath the moon, a silver hue,
A world reborn, a tranquil view.

Breath visible in frosty air,
Moments linger without a care.
The night deepens, shadows play,
In this dreamlike winter's sway.

Wrapped in warmth, we seek retreat,
In the calm, our hearts can meet.
Underneath this blanket bright,
We find peace in winter's night.

Peace of Mind in Winter's Light

Morning breaks with golden rays,
Chasing shadows from the days.
Snowflakes dance in gentle breeze,
Whispers shared among the trees.

The world awakens, fresh and clear,
Filled with warmth, free of fear.
In this light, our worries fade,
Gentle thoughts are serenely laid.

Mountains quiet, draped in white,
A canvas pure, a peaceful sight.
Breath of winter fills the air,
Moments cherished, free of care.

Frosted branches glisten bright,
Nature's beauty, pure delight.
In the stillness, hearts align,
Finding peace in joy divine.

As we gather, hand in hand,
In this wonder, we will stand.
With every heartbeat, love takes flight,
In the peace of winter's light.

Secrets Breathed Out in Chilled Air

In the stillness, secrets shine,
Carried softly, like a sign.
Breathed out gently, thoughts take flight,
In the chill of winter's night.

Frosted whispers, tender sighs,
Hidden truths beneath the skies.
With each breath, we share our dreams,
Woven softly in moonbeams.

In the cold, our spirits rise,
Finding warmth in shared goodbyes.
Voices echo, faint and clear,
In the silence, we draw near.

Nature listens, wise and old,
Tales of love, yet to be told.
In the quiet, hearts confide,
Every secret, love as guide.

Breaths of winter, soft and light,
Gathered hopes glide into the night.
Bonded close in frosty air,
We find solace everywhere.

Effervescent Calm of Winter's Song

Winter's song, a gentle tune,
Sings the heavens and the moon.
In each note, a breath of chill,
Melodies that time will fill.

Softly falling, snowflakes weave,
Whispers of the hearts that grieve.
Yet in beauty, we find mirth,
Through the frost, we know our worth.

Branches sway with quiet grace,
Nature's rhythm, sacred space.
In the echo, dreams unfold,
Beauty found in stories told.

Glimmers dance in icy light,
In this moment, all feels right.
With each heartbeat, calm descends,
In this song, the spirit mends.

In the flurry of the night,
We find warmth, our souls ignite.
Winter's song, a breath of air,
Eases burdens, lifts despair.

The Harmony of Winter's Stillness

Frosted fields lay soft and bright,
Beneath the moon's gentle light.
Whispers of snowflakes dance and glide,
In this calm, we take our stride.

Branches cradle winter's grace,
Slumbering trees in a silent place.
Each breath a cloud in the chilled air,
Nature's magic, precious and rare.

Silent nights, a blanket tight,
Stars twinkle in the crisp twilight.
Footprints leading, soft and slow,
To secret paths where dreams can grow.

In the stillness, hearts entwine,
Finding peace, like aged wine.
Winter's hush, a soothing balm,
Embracing us in quiet calm.

So let us pause, reflect, and share,
The gifts of winter everywhere.
In harmony, we find our way,
Through winter's night to greet the day.

Nature's Silent Symphony

The trees resume their jeweled lace,
Each branch a note in nature's grace.
Softly singing in the breeze,
Harmony found in rustling leaves.

Drifting snowflakes, delicate flight,
Conducting peace in the winter night.
A symphony of silence reigns,
On frosted hills and gentle plains.

Moonlight spills on the frozen lake,
Mirroring stars for nature's sake.
Each ripple plays a quiet song,
Where we feel that we belong.

Crystalline air, sharp and clear,
Whispers of winter draw us near.
In the stillness, hearts align,
Creating beauty by design.

Upon the canvas, night unfolds,
Stories of magic yet untold.
In nature's arms, we find our peace,
In this silent symphony, we cease.

The Whispering White of Winter

A blanket soft, the world in white,
Whispers linger in the night.
Gentle flakes kiss the ground,
In their dance, pure peace is found.

Silhouettes of branches bare,
Dressed in frost, they stand with care.
Echoes of silence fill the air,
As winter's breath cradles us there.

Footsteps muffled, lost to wear,
In the hush, we stop and stare.
Every moment, crisp and bright,
Illuminates the quiet night.

Stars wink down, with secrets kept,
In winter's charm, we are swept.
The whispering white calls us near,
In this season, we hold dear.

So let us linger, hold this sight,
In the whispers of the night.
Together we embrace the chill,
With hearts aglow, a winter thrill.

Reflections in a Crystal Stillness

Mirror lakes in the pale light,
Show the world in stillness bright.
Winter's breath hangs in the air,
Praising beauty, beyond compare.

Each flake a story, crystal spun,
In nature's grasp, we become one.
The night wraps close, a velvet glow,
Enveloping dreams in shimmering snow.

Invisible music fills the night,
Creating calm, a pure delight.
Each reflection whispers low,
In the stillness, time moves slow.

Frosty patterns lace the glass,
Memories linger as they pass.
In this tranquil, frozen peace,
We find a moment's sweet release.

So let us walk where silence reigns,
Through crystal paths on winter's plains.
Each step a dance, each breath a thrill,
In the beauty of this crystal still.

Echoes of Stillness in the Cold

In winter's breath, the world feels near,
Silence whispers soft, devoid of fear.
Branches bow with frosted lace,
Time moves slow in this sacred space.

Footsteps muffled by the snow,
Hearts connect where cold winds blow.
Memories linger in the chill,
Each echo finds a quiet thrill.

Stars peek out from velvet skies,
Reflecting dreams in frozen sighs.
The night wraps all in its embrace,
While shadows dance with gentle grace.

Beneath the quiet, life remains,
Hidden warmth amidst the pains.
Nature's pulse, a steady beat,
In stillness, every heart finds heat.

So let the cold come wrap us tight,
In echo's hold, we'll find the light.
Together here, where spirits bold,
Embrace the echoes, brave and cold.

Silhouettes in a Snowy Hush

Beneath the trees, the shadows play,
Silhouettes dance in a gentle sway.
Snowflakes fall like whispers soft,
Carrying secrets from aloft.

Quiet drapes the world in white,
Nature's canvas, pure delight.
Every branch wears a crystal crown,
In snowy hush, we lay us down.

Footprints trace a hidden path,
Guiding hearts away from wrath.
In this stillness, dreams unfold,
Stories waiting to be told.

Winter moons cast silver light,
Illuminating our shared sight.
Together we tread on frozen ground,
In whispered moments, love is found.

So let us dwell in this serene,
Where winter's magic reigns supreme.
Silhouettes against the snow,
In hush, our hearts begin to glow.

Glimmers of Calm Amidst the Snow

Amidst the flurry, calm prevails,
Glimmers shine where silence sails.
Echoes of peace in every flake,
Softly whispered, hearts awake.

Gentle breezes touch the skin,
Inviting warmth from deep within.
Together under starlit skies,
We'll weave our dreams, unbound, and rise.

Snow-capped hills hold memories dear,
In each still moment, love draws near.
Light refracts in a world so bright,
In glimmering calm, we find our light.

Frozen lakes reflect the stars,
Carving stories, erasing scars.
With every breath, new life is born,
In tranquil resolve, hope is sworn.

Let the chill encircle tight,
In this calm, we'll take our flight.
With glimmers of love amidst the snow,
Together, we'll embrace and grow.

The Silence of Falling Stars

In the night, the world holds its breath,
Stars descend, a dance with death.
Whispers linger in the dark,
Flickers of dreams ignite a spark.

Each falling star, a wish unspooled,
In silence, hearts are gently ruled.
Time slows, as the heavens weep,
In their light, secrets we keep.

Through the void, they paint the skies,
Guiding lost souls with their sighs.
In the stillness, wishes rise,
Crafting hope from starry ties.

Underneath this cosmic show,
Love and wonder begin to flow.
In the silence, fate is spun,
Two hearts whispering, becoming one.

So when you gaze upon the night,
Listen close, and hold on tight.
For in the silence of the stars,
Our dreams converge, no matter how far.

Hearts Reside in Frost-Kissed Corners

In corners where the snowflakes dance,
Hearts whisper dreams, a fleeting glance.
Beneath the frost, old memories lie,
Wrapped in silence, echoes of a sigh.

Each heartbeat soft, a gentle sound,
In winter's grasp, love's warmth is found.
Time stretches thin as shadows blend,
In frosted spaces, hearts transcend.

Crystals form on windows bright,
Illuminating the cold, soft light.
Yet in the chill, a bond ignites,
Amidst the winter's starry nights.

Footprints trace on glistening ground,
Each step a memory tightly wound.
In frosted corners, secrets bloom,
Hearts reside in the winter's room.

As the world sleeps under a blanket white,
Hearts find solace, wrapped up tight.
In the quietude, a promise grows,
In bated breath, the longing flows.

Frost-kissed corners, a sacred space,
Where love, like nature, finds its place.
Here in the stillness, we both belong,
In winter's embrace, our hearts stay strong.

Still Hearts Beneath a White Embrace

Beneath the white, a stillness reigns,
Hearts entwined like gentle chains.
In quiet moments, love persists,
In winter's grasp, no one resists.

Frost-covered branches, a secret kept,
In every glance, the world has slept.
Whispers drift on the icy air,
Still hearts beating, a silent prayer.

The snowflakes fall, soft as a sigh,
Covering hopes as they drift by.
Entwined our dreams, like threads of white,
In the cool embrace of calming night.

Each breath a cloud in the frosty air,
Holding onto moments, tender care.
In winter's hush, our laughter glows,
Still hearts beating where love flows.

Amidst the frost, we find our place,
In tranquil stillness, a warm embrace.
Silent promises beneath the snow,
In winter's light, our love will grow.

So here we stand, together, bold,
In the white embrace, love's story told.
Still hearts nestled in harmony,
In nature's breath, forever free.

The Palette of Quietude in White

Amidst the calm, a world adorned,
The palette white, pure and warmed.
Each shade a hush, a tranquil tone,
In winter's embrace, we're never alone.

Frosted whispers on the breeze,
Painting silence beneath the trees.
With every flake, a story spun,
In this quietude, our hearts have won.

A tapestry of softest dreams,
Crafted in quiet, like gentle streams.
The world slows down, as colors blend,
In frosty hues, our love transcends.

Each step we take, a dance of light,
In snow-kissed moments, pure delight.
Unity shines in every fold,
In the palette white, our love's retold.

With hearts aglow in winter's grace,
Together we find our sacred place.
In the stillness, magic unfolds,
As the palette of quietude consoles.

In the snowy depths, our spirits rise,
In this embrace, where true love lies.
Through every storm, with each soft fall,
The palette of white, loves sweetest call.

Frost-Kissed Whispers of Tranquility

Beneath the frost, a soft refrain,
Whispers linger, love's gentle strain.
In tranquil moments, hearts align,
Wrapped in silence, so divine.

The world holds breath as shadows play,
In crystal cloaks, we find our way.
Frost-kissed whispers, secrets deep,
In quietude, our dreams we keep.

Every flake a promise sweet,
Guiding paths where lovers meet.
In stillness found, we share a glance,
In winter's breath, love's quiet dance.

Gentle echoes in the night,
Frosty breath, a soft delight.
In layered snow, our hopes arise,
Frost-kissed whispers, love's lullabies.

Beneath the stars, the world is hushed,
In snowy blankets, time is crushed.
In tender moments, we take flight,
Frost-kissed whispers, hearts ignite.

As winter wraps its arms around,
In tranquility, we are found.
In every gust, sweet words confer,
Frost-kissed whispers, forever her.

Frosted Memories Under White Skies

Silent whispers fill the air,
Softly drifting, unaware,
Blanket white on every hill,
A moment paused, the world holds still.

Chasing shadows, dreams appear,
Laced with joy and laced with fear,
Footsteps traced in icy sighs,
Frosted memories 'neath white skies.

The chill of winter grips the heart,
Yet warmth ignites, refusing to part,
With every breath, a story shared,
In nature's arms, we are repaired.

Time meanders like the streams,
In frosted glades where silence beams,
Each moment, a cherished sight,
Under the glow of soft, pale light.

Minted wishes in the snow,
A quiet peace where hopes do grow,
Wrapped in dreams both fresh and bright,
Frosted memories shining white.

Silence Between Snowflakes

Gentle flakes descend like sighs,
Caught in quiet, soft the skies,
Each one falls, a silent grace,
Blanketing the bustling place.

Hushed cascades upon the street,
Every step feels soft and sweet,
A world that breathes in purest calm,
Wrapped in winter's soothing balm.

Echoes dance on crisp, cold air,
Whispers float without a care,
In the stillness, hearts unwind,
A gentle touch for peace to find.

Beneath the flakes, the world does pause,
Nature's breath without a cause,
Silence spreads its gentle wings,
In this quiet, the spirit sings.

Moments linger, time extends,
In the frost, a love transcends,
Silence speaks in tender tones,
Between the snowflakes, two hearts known.

A Calm Pulse Beneath the Cold

Frozen echoes through the night,
Yet within, a pulse of light,
Beneath the frost, life gently stirs,
A whisper heard as stillness occurs.

Crystalline dreams in shadows play,
Where warmth hides in the cool array,
Amidst the chill, a fire burns bright,
Calls from within, a quiet delight.

Every flake a story told,
A tapestry of soft and bold,
With every breath, the heart feels whole,
A calm pulse beneath the cold.

Life persists in frozen ground,
In every silence, hope is found,
Hidden treasures, the soul ignites,
In winter's depths, the spirit writes.

Through icy veils, connections flow,
With gentle hearts, we softly show,
That warmth can thrive in nature's hold,
A calm pulse beneath the cold.

Glittering Peace on Frozen Ground

Mirrored skies reflect the night,
Stars aligned in pure delight,
Around us sparkles all around,
In glittering peace on frozen ground.

Each step leaves a crystal kiss,
In the quiet, a fleeting bliss,
Every moment soft and bright,
Shimmers dancing in the light.

Winter brushes nature's face,
In every corner, time and space,
With gentle beauty, hearts are found,
In glittering peace on frozen ground.

Frosty breath hangs in the air,
Echoing dreams, beyond compare,
With every sigh, we feel the flow,
Of nature's rhythm, soft and slow.

Under stars, our worries cease,
In night's embrace, we find our peace,
A world transformed, enchantment crowned,
In glittering peace on frozen ground.